Johann Sebastian Bach

Complete Concertos for Two or More Harpsichords

in Full Score

From the Bach-Gesellschaft Edition

Dover Publications, Inc., *New York*

Contents

Published in Canada by General Publishing Company, Ltd., 30 Lesmill Road, Don Mills, Toronto, Ontario.

Published in the United Kingdom by Constable and Company, Ltd., 3 The Lanchesters, 162–164 Fulham Palace Road, London W6 9ER.

This Dover edition, first published in 1992, is a republication of portions of Vols. 21, 31 and 43 of *Johann Sebastian Bachs Werke*, originally published by the Bach-Gesellschaft, Breitkopf & Härtel, Leipzig, 1875, 1884, 1894.

Manufactured in the United States of America
Dover Publications, Inc., 31 East 2nd Street, Mineola, N.Y. 11501

Library of Congress Cataloging-in-Publication Data

Bach, Johann Sebastian, 1685–1750.
　　[Concertos. Selections.]
　　Complete concertos for two or more harpsichords / Johann Sebastian Bach.—In full score.
　　　1 score.
　　　String orchestra acc.
　　　"A republication of portions of vols. 21, 31, and 43 of Johann Sebastian Bachs Werke, originally published by the Bach-Gesellschaft, Breitkopf & Härtel, Leipzig, 1875, 1884, 1894"—T.p. verso.
　　　Contents: For two harpsichords in C minor, BWV 1060—For two harpsichords in C major, BWV 1061—For two harpsichords in C minor, BWV 1062—For three harpsichords in D minor, BWV 1063—For three harpsichords in C major, BWV 1064—For four harpsichords in A minor, BWV 1065.
　　　ISBN 0-486-27136-6 (pbk.)
　　　1. Concertos (Harpsichords (2)) with string orchestra—Scores. 2. Concertos (Harpsichords (3)) with string orchestra—Scores. 3. Concertos (Harpsichords (4)) with string orchestra—Scores.
　　M1110.B25　1992　　　　　　　　　　　　92-750349
　　　　　　　　　　　　　　　　　　　　　　　　　CIP
　　　　　　　　　　　　　　　　　　　　　　　　　M

Concerto for Two Harpsichords in C Minor

BWV 1060

Adagio.

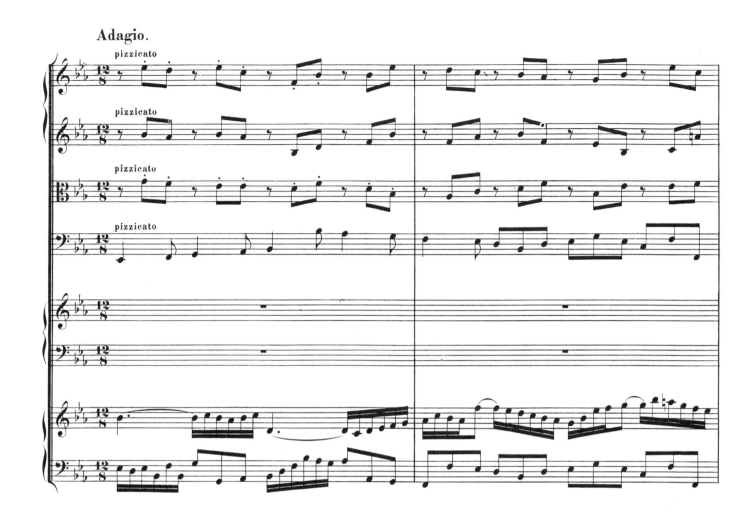

Concerto for Two Harpsichords in C Minor

Concerto for Two Harpsichords in C Major

BWV 1061

Concerto for Two Harpsichords in C Major

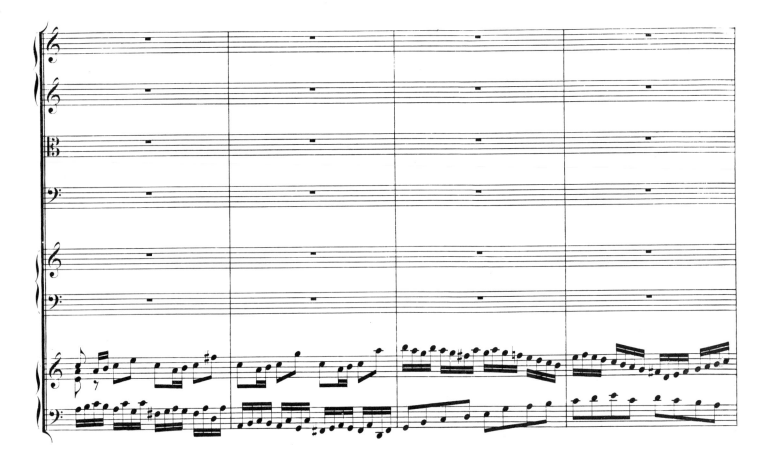

Concerto for Two Harpsichords in C Major

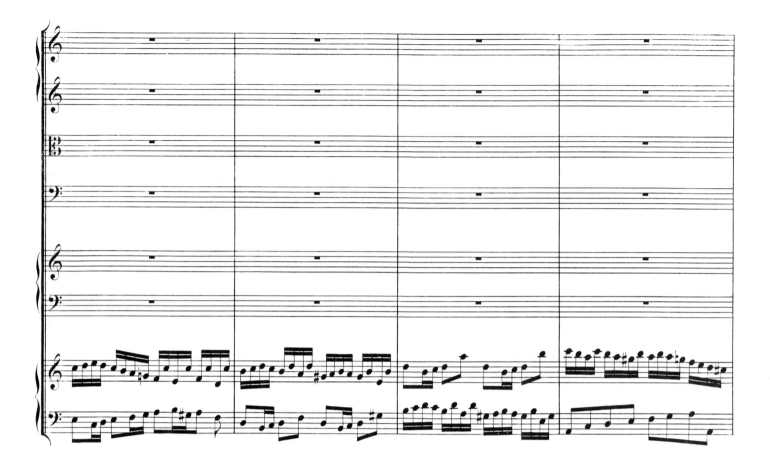

Concerto for Two Harpsichords in C Major

Adagio ovvero Largo. (Quartetto tacet)

Concerto for Two Harpsichords in C Major

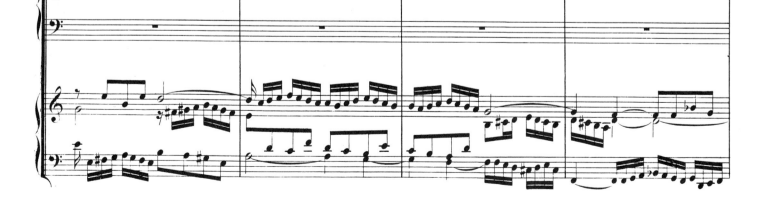

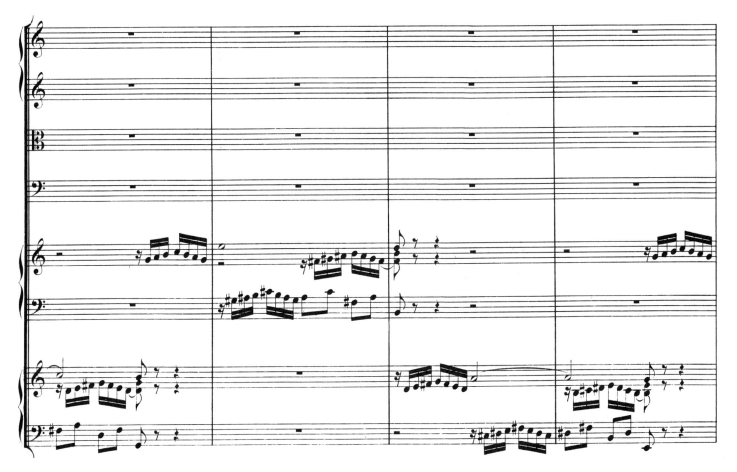

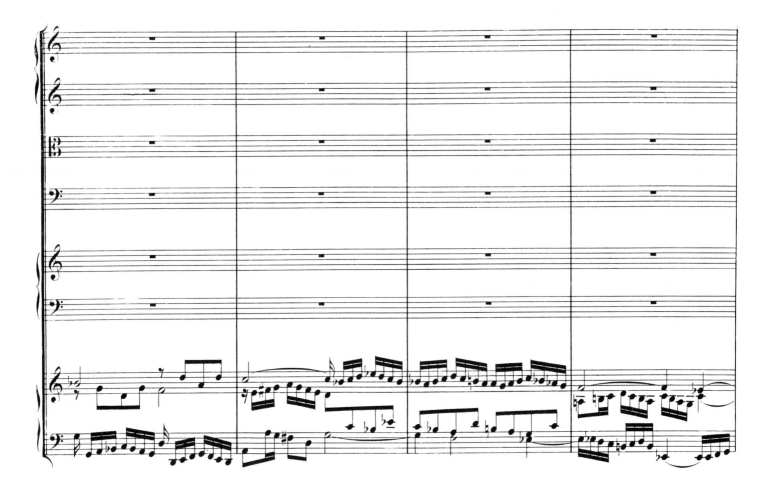

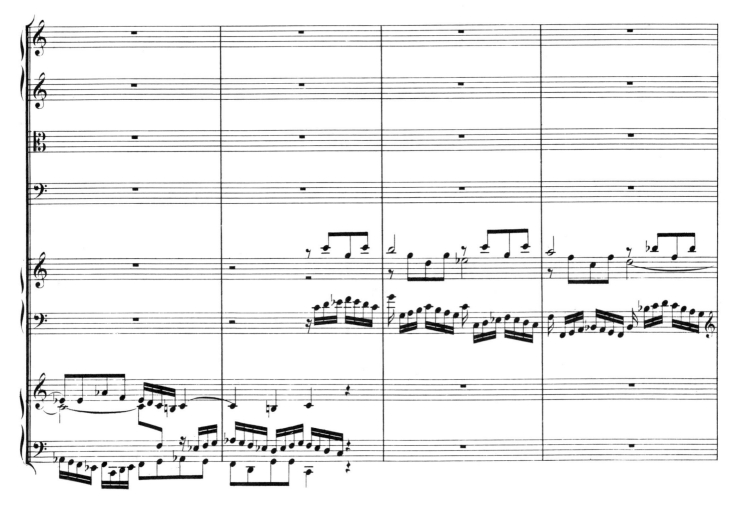

Concerto for Two Harpsichords in C Minor

BWV 1062

⊕ ⊕ oder ∽?

⊕ oder ∽?

Allegro assai.

Concerto for Two Harpsichords in C Minor

Concerto for Two Harpsichords in C Minor

⊕ oder ⅲ ?

Concerto for Three Harpsichords in D Minor

BWV 1063

Concerto for Three Harpsichords in D Minor

122 *Concerto for Three Harpsichords in D Minor*

Concerto for Three Harpsichords in D Minor

Alla Siciliana.
forte
staccato
forte
staccato
forte
staccato
forte
forte
forte
forte
tr
piano
piano
forte
piano
piano

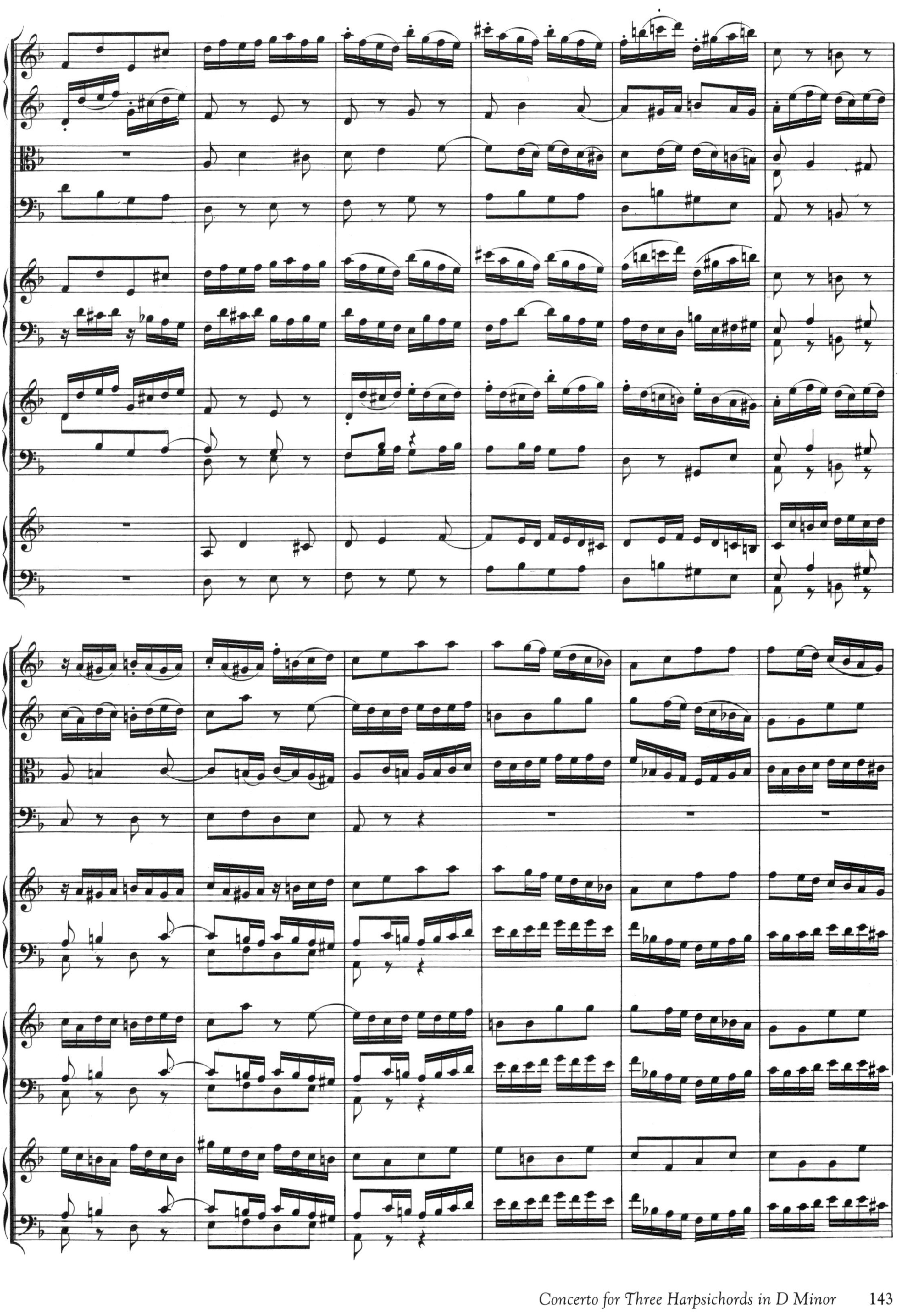

Concerto for Three Harpsichords in D Minor

154   *Concerto for Three Harpsichords in D Minor*

Concerto for Three Harpsichords in D Minor

Concerto for Three Harpsichords in C Major

BWV 1064

Concerto for Three Harpsichords in C Major

Concerto for Three Harpsichords in C Major

Concerto for Three Harpsichords in C Major

Concerto for Three Harpsichords in C Major

Concerto for Three Harpsichords in C Major

Concerto for Three Harpsichords in C Major

Concerto for Three Harpsichords in C Major

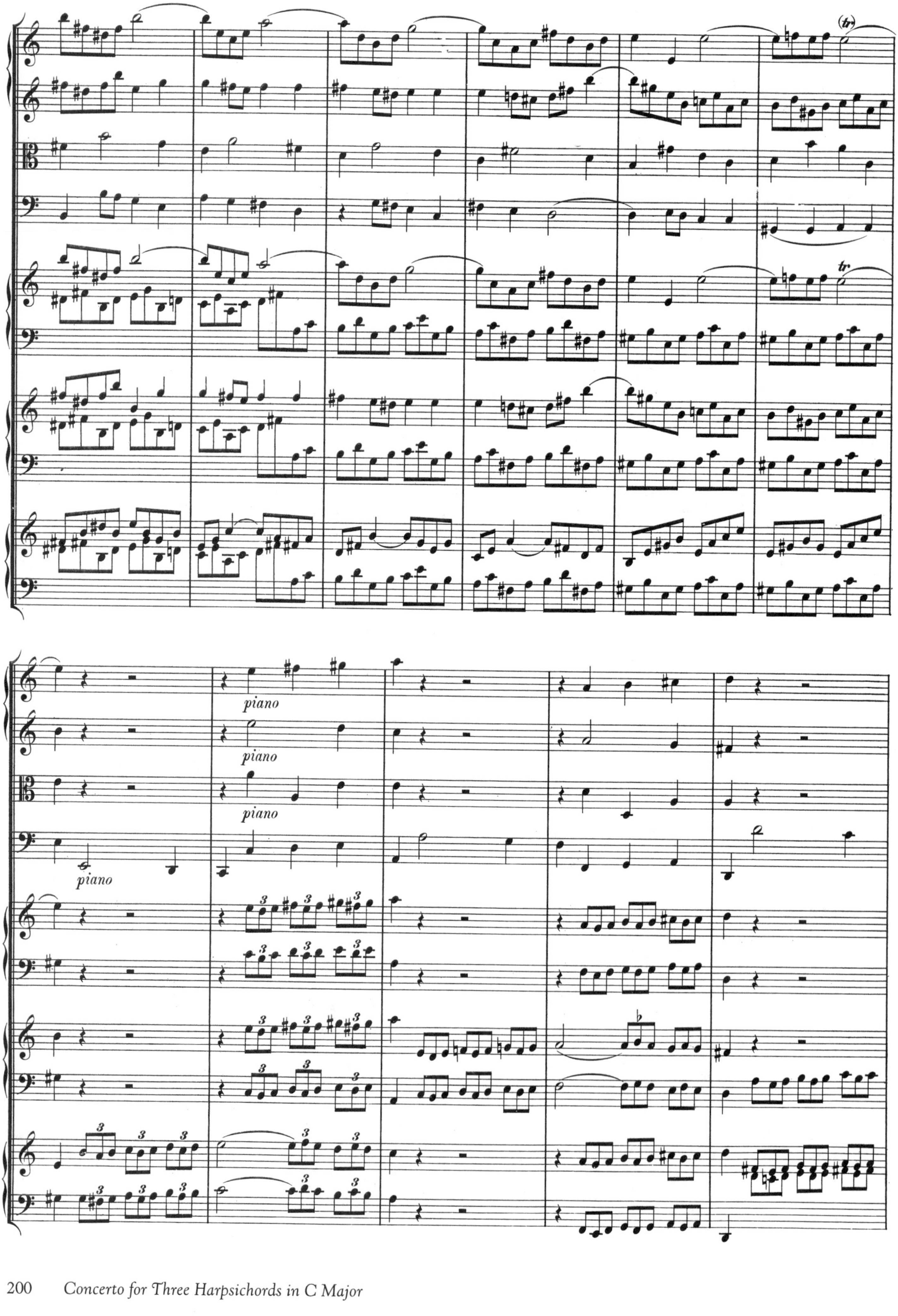
(tr)
tr
piano
piano
piano
piano

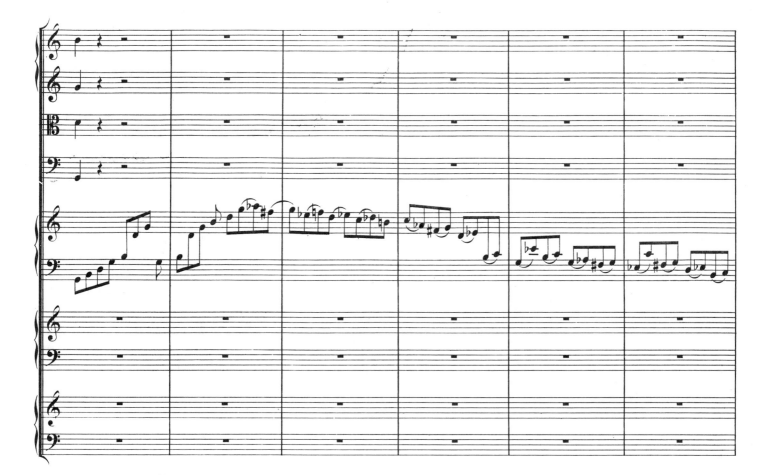

Concerto for Four Harpsichords in A Minor

BWV 1065

Concerto for Four Harpsichords in A Minor

Largo.

Concerto for Four Harpsichords in A Minor

Concerto for Four Harpsichords in A Minor

Concerto for Four Harpsichords in A Minor

Concerto for Four Harpsichords in A Minor

END

Concerto for Four Harpsichords in A Minor